Wind that Fans the Flame

Flo Ellers

Copyright © 2013 Dr. Flo Ellers

ISBN: 978-0-942507-46-1

ISBN (E-BOOK): 978-0-942507-40-9

All rights reserved. No part of this publication may be reproduced, stored in a retrieval system, or transmitted in any form or by any means—electronic, mechanical, photocopy, or any other—except for brief quotations in printed reviews, without permission in writing from the publisher and/or author.

Unless otherwise noted, all scripture references are from the New King James Version. Copyright © 1982 by Thomas Nelson, Inc. Used by permission. All rights reserved.

Address all personal correspondence to:
Dr. Flo Ellers
PO Box 8061
Lacey, WA 98509-8061

Email: floellers153@gmail.com

Individuals and church groups may order books from Dr. Flo Ellers directly, or from the publisher. Retailers and wholesalers should order from our distributors. Refer to the Deeper Revelation Books website for distribution information, as well as an online catalog of all our books.

Published by:
Deeper Revelation Books
Revealing "the deep things of God" (1 Cor. 2:10)
P.O. Box 4260
Cleveland, TN 37320
423-478-2843
Website: www.deeperrevelationbooks.org
Email: info@deeperrevelationbooks.org

Deeper Revelation Books assists Christian authors in publishing and distributing their books. Final responsibility for design, content, permissions, editorial accuracy, and doctrinal views, either expressed or implied, belongs to the author.

FOREWORD
by Pastor Guy C. Carey

The testimony of Jesus is the spirit of prophecy. When we share the marvelous works of Christ in our lives we release faith in the lives of those who hear, so it is with *Wind that Fans the Flame*. Flo Ellers shares her spiritual journey of defeat and victory, mountain tops and valleys, the sorrows and joys of following Jesus Christ. Your soul will identify with some part of her adventure in God. As you read this testimony open your heart to the *Wind that Fans the Flame*.

In a season of prayer in preparation for ministry in Northern Minnesota, I was given a picture of a person rapidly being transported from Native American reservation to reservation. Everywhere this entity went there was a major outpouring of God's Holy Spirit. The Native Church was revived and fire of revival spread to many. As I shared this with my prayer partners at the time, one of them came forth with an insight from God. I would meet a Native person on this trip and I was to give them a new name; that name was *"Wind that Fans the Flame."*

Twenty years ago, 2000 miles from my home in a dining hall in the backwoods of Minnesota, the conversation with my traveling companion went something like this. "Guy, what do you think? Flo Ellers is the only Native American here. Do you think she is the one?" "I do not know, David. Why don't you ask her if she has an Indian name?" David promptly and boldly marched over to the table where the attractive Native woman sat with her friends.

Interrupting their conversation with a polite, however naively insensitive question, he asked, "Pardon me madam, do you have an Indian name?" Her reply came quickly, "Yes, but I have laid it aside and I am waiting for the Lord to change my name!" Without stopping to converse, David excitedly returned to our table to announce, "She's the one! She has an Indian name and she is waiting for God to change her name. You need to tell her!"

Just as we were speaking, Flo and all her friends showed up at our table with puzzled looks and questions. With intense interest Flo asked why we were making inquiries of her. Looking up at her I had an inner urgency to say, "Flo, I have a word for you from God given to me in my living room in prayer before traveling here. I am to give you a new name. From this day forth you shall be known as *Wind that Fans the Flame*. The Spirit of God is mighty upon you and He shall blow you from place to place with haste. Wherever you go the fire of revival will go with you especially among Native American people."

The Holy Spirit is the *Flame and the Wind* but He chooses vessels to carry His life, fire, wind and word to a lost and dying world bound by sin and death. Flo Ellers is such a vessel and her testimony is the testimony of Jesus who desires to ignite your heart as you read *Wind that Fans the Flame*.

Grace to you as you find yourself in these pages. May you find hope that no matter how dark it is in your world, there is One who loves you and will ignite your soul with His Spirit!

> Pastor Guy C. Carey
> Pastor Immanuel's Church
> Silver Spring, Maryland

TABLE OF CONTENTS

CHAPTER 1
Warrior Child Of The Tlingit Indians 9

CHAPTER 2
Santa Claus Is Coming To Town 17

CHAPTER 3
An Outpouring Of Signs,
Wonders And Miracles 21

CHAPTER 4
Nobody Loves A Drunken Indian 27

CHAPTER 5
Anchorage Psychiatric Institute 31

CHAPTER 6
My Battle With The Forces Of Witchcraft 41

CHAPTER 7
My Call Into Full Time Ministry 51

CHAPTER 8
The Last Days Church 57

CHAPTER 1

WARRIOR CHILD OF THE TLINGIT INDIANS

The "People Of The Tides"

Many years ago, my Tlingit people used to travel by canoe from their home village of Klukwan to their summer camps of Hole-In-The-Wall, Tuxekan and Klawock to put up their winter supply of food. The salmon, deer, seals and berries were so plentiful around the Prince of Wales Island off the coast of SE Alaska the "People of the Tides," the Tlingits, decided to make Klawock their permanent home.

The Tlingits have two main social groups—the Eagle and the Raven. These divide into several clans and the clans are subdivided into house groups. These groups have crests displayed on their totem poles, their jewelry, weavings, feast dishes and other art forms. My family were Ravens from the Gaan-ax-adi (phonetically) Clan and the Mink House. Our people were strict on identity so we would not intermarry.

On the highest hill in Klawock, the villagers erected 21 totem poles carried from the village of Tuxekan. The city built a carving shed to house the poles during the restoration of the totems. Each totem pole told a story of some notable event, or a clan's lineage, or a cultural belief.

Our people show respect to the animals carved on the poles because they believe they have a spirit. They also show respect to the live animals because they believe they could be the spirit of a reincarnated ancestor.

My people usually had large families so every summer the entire family worked long tiring hours preparing the winter's supply of food and wood for the living room stove. The men would go on their boats far out into the Pacific Ocean to get sea gull eggs, King Salmon, and seals. In the fall, they would hunt for deer and occasionally bring home a swan or ducks. Even though Grandpa and my Uncle Johnnie would use a blowtorch to scorch off the ducks' feathers, the duck soup Grandma made still tasted good. The women would go on the beach, pick seaweed, and spread it on white cloth covered tables in the hot sun to dry. Though we were very young children, we did our share of the hard work. We would be grinding up some of the seaweed in food grinders until midnight with our heads bobbing from lack of sleep … but it was all right, for this was necessary for our survival in the cold, harsh winter months.

Our people are typically short and stocky and very strong including the women and children. When Grandpa and Uncle Johnnie would saw a fallen tree with their chainsaw, they would split the wood and all the girls in the family would stack the wood into piles under the house. Grandpa took a 50-gallon drum and turned it into a stove. In winter, he would fill it up with wood. That made our house so warm, but by midnight, the wood was ashes and the house was cold again. Grandma made quilts from the coats she bought from the Goodwill Store and piled 6-8 quilts on top of us. In the morning, we had to get water from the outside faucet and fill the basin to wash our faces. The water was so cold, but the smell of breakfast coming from the kitchen moved us quickly along as we washed and got dressed for our first meal of the day.

Grandma usually made us oatmeal or cornmeal mush. Sometimes we had oatmeal with sugar and sometimes just oatmeal. Grandma saved the burnt rice from the pot from the previous night's dinner that she had been soaking and scrapped it all together with the oatmeal and leftover mush into a pan and added cinnamon, raisins, sugar, canned Carnation milk, and if we had it, a couple of eggs, and served this yummy, hot cinnamon dessert after our dinner.

Saturdays were our washing, scrubbing and bath days. Early in the morning, we would go outside on our porch, turn the faucet on, fill our buckets with water, and put it on the kitchen stove. As soon as the water started to boil, we would pour the hot water into our wringer washing machine and start the laundry.

In the afternoon, we would heat more water to scrub our floors. We would use a big deck brush to scrub the wooden planks and when Grandma thought it was clean, we would push the dirty water into the cracks and let it run under the house. Usually one of my jobs was to clean our outhouse. I would fill a basin with water, put some Lysol in it, carry it to our outhouse (toilet), and use a brush to scrub the surface.

Grandma would peel an orange and put the rind on top of the barrel stove and the entire house filled with a beautiful citrus fragrance. Finally, the work was finished and after dinner, Grandma would heat more buckets of water and fill the galvanized tub so we could take a bath. I was always competitive and would usually be the first one in the tub because I never wanted to be the last one in that same water.

Around 11:30 at night, Grandma would fill all the lamps with kerosene and clip the wicks if they were too long, so they would not smoke when she lit the lamps. Right at midnight, the city generators would shut down for the night and the entire village was clothed in darkness until early morning. Just as soon as the lights went out, a pack of dogs would gather almost nightly at the restoration shed at the base of Totem Pole Park and would howl, sending shivers down our back. Once, when the lights went off "someone" was knocking at my bedroom window and the window was at least 8 feet high from the foundation of our house! I was so petrified with fear that the perspiration was running down the side of my face, but I just could not move to wipe the sweat off. When the morning sun peeked over the mountain, and I could hear my Grandma interceding in prayer for us, I knew all was well again.

Roberta is my first cousin, but she was more like a twin sister to me. She is coy and very pretty with two deep dimples in her cheeks that she inherited from our Grandmother. Roberta and I always seemed to be together so when I did something wrong, she was a co-conspirator, mostly an unwilling one, but nonetheless a cousin in crime. When Grandma would send us to Frank's Store to buy something and Frank had to go in the back room to get the item, I was always very quick to steal some candy, just as soon as he turned his back. That stolen Frappe candy bar always tasted sweeter than the candy Grandma gave us. Grandma would go to the store and buy a small bag of penny candy, she would shake the bag to the beat of an Indian song, and we had to Indian dance before she would give us our candy.

In whatever game we played, my cousin, Roberta, told me, I was always the "fearless leader," the head of "the gang." When we played Cowboys and Indians, all the town kids met on the playground or up at the Totem Pole Park. After I organized the "gang," I somehow always managed to be the Indian Princess, "Tiger Lily." My gang would pull me through the town in an old rusty red wagon with two empty canned fish boxes that I sat in. Peering through the cut out windows of the regal coach, "Tiger Lily" was surveying her land and strategizing how to beat those Cowboys to bring about a great victory for the Tlingit Indians.

One sunny afternoon I went alone to play by the area just below the Totem Pole Park. The wind was softly blowing and I felt so free twirling around and around, until I fell on my back onto the stony ground. While gazing up at the curious formation of white clouds, all of a sudden, I became aware someone was watching me. At that moment, I knew it was a Being in the sky, but I did not know who He was and why He was so intently looking at me.

Wind That Fans The Flame

CHAPTER 2

SANTA CLAUS IS COMING TO TOWN

The Community Hall

The trees were turning beautiful shades of faded green, yellow and orange as the cold, fall air whistled through the barren Salmonberry branches. Every fall, Bob put toys in his storefront window encouraging the town people to start saving for their holiday gifts. One day as I walked past the window, I saw the most beautiful, brown-haired bridal doll complete with her white gown and a lace veil on her head. Her beauty astounded me. Every day I would go past Bob's store and spend a few minutes starring at the doll. One day as I did my usual walk, to my utter disappointment, the doll was gone. I had this strange sadness of soul as if I had lost my best friend. From that day on, I no longer went for my daily walk past Bob's store.

Christmas was always a very special time of year for my Grandmother Elizabeth. Grandma was a cheerful giver and had a big heart of love for the lonely children of Klawock and the town's alcoholics. Every Christmas, she found an outlet for that love when she would take some of her precious savings to purchase nuts in the shell, apples, oranges and penny candy. She would put them in brown paper bags and Grandpa Isaac would take them down to the community hall for the evening's gala event. Santa was coming to town!

When you walked into the hall, you could smell the smoked fish sandwiches, my Auntie Alicia's famous lemon meringue pie, cakes smothered in vanilla frosting and all the delectable goodies the women of the village prepared for the town feast.

In the middle of the hall was a spectacular 20-foot Christmas tree decorated with sparkling balls of every size and color, bubbling lights and a paper chain. Everybody was chatting, laughing, eating, and just enjoying the moment when all of a sudden there was a loud banging coming from the direction of the front doors. I was startled with fear and my heart was racing fast, when the banging came again, this time even louder!

One of the town leaders went to the door, opened it, and to our relief and delightful surprise, in came Santa Claus bearing armloads of gifts. When each child's name was called out, they would give an enthusiastic "Over here!", and a gift was given to them. Name after name, Santa yelled out, and looking I saw the gifts almost gone. I felt my heart starting to sink when I heard, "Florence Gannon." I yelled out, and Santa came over to me and gave me a very big box. I grabbed the box and with gleeful excitement tore the Christmas wrapping off, and there she was ... my beautiful brown-haired bridal doll. That was the most exciting Christmas ever! The next day a package came in the mail from our full-blooded Cherokee grandmother, Florence, who lived near Jackson, Mississippi. Every Christmas she always remembered us with gifts. My sister and I anxiously stood by as our Mother opened the gifts. There was a stuffed animal for my younger sister and one for me. In the Christmas card was a photo of my half-brother, Norman, Jr., and a letter to my Mom but there was nothing from our Father.

My father, Norman, was a half-breed, half Irish and half Cherokee. He was very handsome, incredibly strong and loved to fight when he was drinking. When he became a man, he had a wandering spirit and would hop the trains in Mississippi and just go with no destination in mind.

One day he found himself in Washington State, so he decided to fly from Seattle to Ketchikan, Alaska. He took a job as a logger at Edna Bay Camp. When he would need a break from logging, he would go to Ketchikan to get drunk. That is where he met my beautiful Tlingit mother, Cleo. As soon as they got married, my Mother was pregnant with me.

When I was nine months old, my parents took me with them on a fishing trawler along with a deck hand named Willie Jackson. Willie was teaching my Dad how to fish when they noticed smoke coming from the lower level by the bunks. Trapped in the fire, Mom was not able to see the door because of the heavy black smoke so she put my head under a blanket and screamed for help. With quick wit, Willie ran towards the flames, doused a blanket covering his head, grabbed me, put my head under his jacket, and dragged my Mom out by the arm. He again ran below grabbing his mattress and smothered the fire. No boat wanted to come to our rescue because they thought our boat was about to blow up.

After that incident, my parents' relationship deteriorated from the constant bickering and heavy drinking, so my Father left and went back to Mississippi but not before my Mother was pregnant with his second daughter. Mom struggled to raise her children and to provide for us, but she was only a child herself. She became quickly frustrated at being a mother so she gave us to our Grandmother and left for Ketchikan. Without father or mother, I became despondent and withdrew into a cruel world of loneliness.

CHAPTER 3

AN OUTPOURING OF SIGNS, WONDERS AND MIRACLES

Revival Comes to the Prince of Wales Island

In 1934, the United States Congress awarded federal funding for the expansion of the existing fish cannery on the condition that Klawock remain a liquor-free community. Prosperity was evident everywhere as the "People of the Tides" fished and canned their Sockeye and Coho salmon for sale. Japan sent in workers to harvest the fish roe and paid top dollar for the delicacy. Filipinos came and worked in the cannery.

There was joy in the town as the wealth of the land caused many to be successful, until fishermen from other parts of Alaska and the "Lower 48" came to rape the land of its resources and brought in the demon drink of alcohol. The Presbyterian Church where the Christmas Cantata singers once performed to a capacity crowd was now almost empty on Sunday mornings as the people stayed home nursing a hangover. Gradually, morality declined giving way to poverty, violence and child neglect. The once proud community now covered in an atmosphere of darkness, cried out for a deliverer. They struggled for freedom from drinking and wanted peace in their homes once again, but the vicious cycle of defeat continued year after year.

It was during this time of struggle that the Lord gave a night vision to a missionary in Montana named Grace Henysel. The vision spanned 100 years showing the epic struggle of the Tlingits to find deliverance. In her vision, Sis. Henysel saw how the People of the Tides' leader told the people of Klawock that "Dee Kee on Kow" (The Tlingit name of God the Father) has a son whose name is "Dee Kee on Kow do Yeet" (God's Son, Jesus). He further told them His Son loves the Tlingits very much. He died for them on a cross, and He promises that all who will obey Him, will at the close of life, be taken to a home above the stars to live with Him forever.

When the vision ended, she and her husband, Leroy, and their daughter, Judy, with the sanction of their church board, left their home and headed to the Prince of Wales Island. After arriving and settling in for the winter, Sis. Henysel was walking down a packed ice walkway when she came upon a drunken man passed out in the snow. She pointed to him and said, "Lord, I claim this man as my first convert." With that, she went home and told her husband what happened and went into deep prayer for the community of Craig and Klawock.

During the third night of prayer, the Lord spoke to Sis. Henysel and told her to look at her hands. They were dripping with oil from heaven. He told her this would be a sign to the people that there is a God in heaven and He has come down to deliver them. Bro. and Sis. Henysel called for a meeting at the Filipino Hall and slowly the people started attending the meetings. During one of the meetings, the oil again appeared on Sis. Henysel's hands and then it appeared on all the people in attendance!

One night, over the pulpit, a strange blue flame appeared, then it went onto the roof of the place of meeting and then the pillar of fire appeared over every true Christian's home in the community. As Bro. and Sis. Henysel watched in stunned wonder, the flames gathered together and appeared as a band of angels, in white robes. Sis. Henysel said she was speechless as they watched the angels slowly ascend back to heaven.

There were multiple miracles in both churches of Klawock and Craig, such as the raising of the dead and the healing of cancer. The fire from heaven touched every community on the island.

One night, the power of the Lord came into the service and several of the young children were slain in the spirit, and lay on the floor with hands uplifted speaking in a heavenly language. I was one of those children and I heard my Uncle Theodore say to his wife, Alicia, "I think they are speaking Russian." Those were the happiest days of my life.

In 1954, the revival had been going on for a couple of years, when we had a visiting speaker who was also a prophet of the Lord. His name was Bro. Sears. At the conclusion of his message, he opened the altar area for the people to come up for prayer. My Grandmother took my sister and me to the altar and pushed us in front of Bro. Sears. She said, "Pray for these girls. They are going back to live with their Mother and she is a drunk." Bro. Sears laid his hands on our heads and began to speak prophetically saying, "When these girls grow up, they will preach the Gospel." I was nine years old when the Lord called me through Bro. Sears to preach the Word of God to the next generation.

One of the last revival meetings I attended was one I shall never forget. During the high praises, the Holy Spirit filled each of us with a joy unspeakable and full of God's glory. After the high and jubilant praise, the atmosphere slowly changed and we could sense a holy Presence, so we worshipped the Lord Jesus with uplifted hands. Caught up in the ecstasy of worship, I suddenly became aware that my hands were on fire. It felt like two red-hot stove pokers were burning holes in my hands. I reverently opened my eyes, and slowly turned my hands so my palms were facing me. I then looked around to see if any one saw my hands, but no one paid attention to me for they were also worshipping the Lord in the spirit of holiness. I gingerly brought my arms down and never told anyone about my experience. I pondered it and kept it in my heart, not fully understanding the experience, but one etched in my memory for all time.

Wind That Fans The Flame

CHAPTER 4

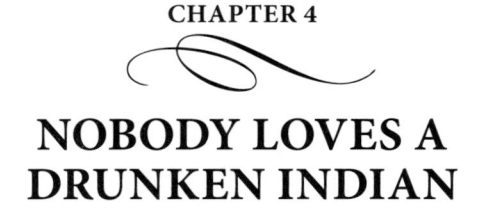

NOBODY LOVES A DRUNKEN INDIAN

Eleven Years of Darkness

After seven years had passed, my life had descended into a terrible condition. "I hate you!" I snarled at the police officer. "Leave me alone you, #*%# *#%^#! I said, leave me alone!" I pulled out of his grip and with clenched fists, I drew my arm back to strike him, but he blocked my punch and twisted my arm behind me, then snapped on the cuffs. He drove me to the jail. The officer on duty called my Mother to the station because they could not constrain me. When I saw her, I became livid with rage. I screamed vulgar profanities repeatedly at her, so the officer told Mom they would have to keep me in jail overnight. My Mother never said a word as she walked away from me with lowered head in painful silence.

Two officers took the cuffs off and with great difficulty; they put me in a faded white, strait jacket. As I lay on the filthy mattress, I lifted up my head and in the faint darkness; I saw small, black, crawling spiders all over the top of my cell. I did not know it at the time, but I was in full-blown delirium tremors (DT's), but the spiders looked very real to me.

All of a sudden, a dark terrorizing spirit of fear gripped me as I looked helplessly at them. I screamed out for help, but no one came. Now the black spiders were multiplying so fast that my entire cell was covered with them. With determination, I struggled to get up and somehow I got out of the strait jacket! The spiders grew in size and they filled my cell with their eerie, evil presence. Again, I doubled up my fists, started hitting the spiders that clung to the steel bars with my bare hands until my hands swelled beyond recognition, and were black from congealed blood.

In the morning as I awakened I remembered that day was a "special" day: it was my birthday … I was 16 years old.

It was the first day of school and during the lunch period, cliques were already forming—the Whites with the Whites and the Alaskan Natives with the Alaskan Natives. I sat next to my newly found friend and saw a name scribbled on her notebook, so I asked her who Mike Ellers was and she pointed in his direction. There were at least five Natives drawn to Mike so I said whoever gets the first date with him wins five dollars.

That night all of us gathered at the Teen Age Club to dance the Mashed Potato and the Twist and do some drinking if we could get some booze. Drinking gave us false confidence that masked our feelings of inferiority when the Whites were around. Even at the Teen Club, there was a racial line, but I noticed Mike strolling and talking with friends on both sides of the club. I liked that. When the club was closing and we all gathered outside, I walked up to Mike and asked him if he would like to go out with me. He smiled at me with his deep blue eyes and said, "Yes."

His easygoing style and gentle nature was attractive to me. I never won the five dollars, but I won Mike. During our first date, I found out his father had just passed away, and his family was from Russia. I shared with him where I was from and that I never knew a Father's love so our similar losses seemed to bring solace to us that bonded us together. On our third date, Mike gently kissed me and I had an unknown feeling that I had never experienced, but it went deep and pure. We were in love.

Wind That Fans The Flame

CHAPTER 5

ANCHORAGE PSYCHIATRIC INSTITUTE (API)

You're Going to Make it This Time!

"Mike!" I screamed in terror, "The demons are tormenting me. Mike, please help me! Please help me!" Mike ran past our four daughters, grabbed the phone and called the ambulance. The Health Aides came, picked me up, and put me on a stretcher. They drove quickly to the emergency room of St. Ann's Hospital in Juneau, where the doctor admitted me. After a preliminary exam, the doctor spoke to Mike and said I needed further treatment, so I flew to Anchorage and went to the Psychiatric Institute.

The doctors put me on several drugs to subdue me, which made me feel like a zombie. Then the nurses took me to a gray, windowless room that had padded walls and a mattress on the floor and warned me if I became violent, this was the room they would put me in. The psychiatrists interrogated me with many questions and had me do a test looking at black splotches and telling them what I see. With each day, I was getting angrier, but the drugs they administered to me kept me from becoming violent.

I felt so alone. It was a horrible place. I slowly looked around the room, a large woman was standing naked and doing horrible things with her body, and another young woman with vacant eyes was walking up and down the hallway with clenched fists hitting the wall repeatedly with a placid look on her face. I quickly left that room and hid in my cubicle. I thought they must be giving her the same drugs they were giving to me.

I was trailing off to sleep when I heard a woman's beautiful voice, so I crawled out of bed and peeked around the corner. There I saw a short, plump nurse with a radiant face quietly singing, "Put your hand in the hand of the Man who stilled the waters, put your hand in the hand of the Man of Galilee … ," I knew that song. That song was about Jesus. "J-E-S-U-S," I whispered softly. I had not heard that name since I left Klawock in 1960. I peeked at her again and wondered how she could have such joy at midnight, in a psyche ward, with all of us to watch? I went back to bed and immediately fell into a deep sleep.

Suddenly, I could feel myself being hurled down into a black hole and I was scrapping the sides with my fingernails trying to find a ledge or something poking out of that dark cylinder but I could not find anything to grab. Then I felt the warmth, now it was getting hotter and hotter and I could hardly breathe in the hot air. I started panicking as the downward pull became stronger than my strength to break the fall. I could feel the hot flames licking up for my feet. I knew where I was ... in hell.

Then I heard my Grandmother's booming voice yelling at me. Suddenly she grabbed my wrist with such force she stopped me from falling. I heard her say with great tenderness, "Florence, you're going to make it this time!" Before her words fully penetrated my mind, I heard another sound: the crack of thunder. It was so loud it startled me. I looked up in the direction of the peal of thunder and saw these white clouds quickly pulled back from side to side ... then I saw Jesus sitting on His regal throne ... and I knew He was coming for me.

The following morning I spoke to the head nurse and shared my night vision with her and I added, "Nobody can help me now, only Jesus." She told the head doctor and a meeting was scheduled for that afternoon. I walked into the conference room. There were doctors and nurses sitting around a wood table, and they asked me to tell them about my dream. I shared it with them and declared with firmness, "Nobody can help me, but God." I then added, "I want to go home." They said even if they could start the process to let me go home, it would take at least a week of "red tape." Long story, short, I was back home in Juneau in 48 hours.

The first Sunday home, I went to Bethel Assembly of God on Fourth and Franklin. I heard the pastor tell the story of the woman caught in adultery. As I was listening to him, my face became red with shame and I quickly looked around to see if anyone was staring at me. Everyone was intently listening to the story about Jesus' love and forgiveness. I liked what I heard, so I went again the following Sunday night, then again for the third Sunday in a row.

This time the church was packed to capacity to hear this Presbyterian evangelist named George Ottis. When Mr. Ottis went to the pulpit, he was speaking in a soft tone, not like the fiery style of the pastor. I cannot tell you what he preached but when he gave the altar call, I indicated with the others that I, too, wanted the offer of salvation. Mr. Ottis told the seekers they did not have to come to the altar area but they could just stand where they were and repeat after him. As I repeated each sentence of his prayer, my tears were flowing unashamedly onto my green wool dress. While I was praying, suddenly a bright light appeared in front of me. It was like the light of a 20,000-watt bulb. I started trembling and weeping as I repeated each sentence after him.

Father in heaven, I come to You in the Name of Your Son, Jesus, who shed His blood on the cross for me. Jesus, I confess to You, I am a sinner. I ask You to forgive me of all my sins. I believe You died for me. I believe You shed Your blood for me. I believe You rose from the dead for me. I ask You to be my Savior. I renounce Satan as my master and I make You my only Lord and Redeemer. I ask you now to give me the assurance that I am truly born again. Then if I should die, I know I will be in heaven with you for all eternity. Thank you, Jesus, for saving me and making me Your child.

When we finished the prayer of salvation, the Light that was standing in front of me came into my being, and Jesus and my spirit were now one.

Then Jesus spoke to them again, saying, "I am the light of the world. He who follows Me shall not walk in darkness, but have the light of life." (John 8:12)

Then the evangelist said if anyone wants to receive the Baptism in the Holy Spirit, meet me in the back room. I quickly turned and ran down the church aisle shouting, "Oh, Hallelujah!" Just the day before, I had screamed at my children using nasty four-letter words... now I was shouting "Hallelujah!" Something wonderful has just happened to me!

There were around 35 assembled in the prayer room, mostly Native Americans. Mr. Ottis began by expounding the Scriptures related to the Holy Spirit. With each verse he shared, it was as if I was being pumped up with helium. I did not know what that was. It is called faith. After about 20 minutes of Scriptures and instruction, he said, "Now I want you to raise your hands and begin to praise the Lord. However, I do not want you to say one word of English or use your Native language."

We raised our hands as instructed and began to say words of adoration to Jesus in a spiritual language we had never learned. Then he said, "Stop!" We did. Then he encouraged us to adore the Lord again, we did, and it was the same spiritual language flowing from our lips. He told us we could start and stop when we want to. My heart was bursting with love for Jesus. The joy I felt was the same joy I experienced as a child in that small church in Klawock.

He dismissed us and I ran home to tell Mike what had just happened to me. Then I went to the bathroom, opened the medicine cabinet and unscrewed each bottle of drugs the API doctors had given to me and flushed them down the toilet. As I did so, I sang, "Thank you, Lord, for saving my soul. Thank you, Lord, for making me whole. Thank you, Lord, for giving to me, Thy great salvation so rich and free."

Shortly thereafter, I ran into a Catholic businessman who owned a small grocery store and I stopped to speak to him. I told him who I was and shared with him my salvation experience. While I shared, he was staring at me as if he was unable to speak. I told him I used to go to his store and steal many food items so I could feed my children. I testified I did not have any money because I used our money on booze and street drugs. Then I put my hand in my pocket and gave him almost all the money I had and added, "I think that will pay back all that I stole from you." As I walked away from him, he said a meek "Thank you" with this bewildered look on his face, but I went away rejoicing.

Every time the church doors opened, I was there with my family. One Wednesday service the pastor said it was time to give our tithes and offerings to the Lord. I asked the Lord how much He wanted me to give to Him. He said, "Put your hand in your pocket and whatever your hand can grab, put it in the offering plate." That day, I had cashed my check from my first job and put the money in my pocket. I thought, "Put your big hand in your big pocket and grab?" Well, I did as the Lord said, and because of my obedience, I have lived a very blessed and favored life since giving that offering so many years ago.

Today, I still give my monthly 10% in tithes and in addition to my 10%, I have given freewill offerings in every service I attend with the exception of one or two. In fact, over the 42 years I have been a believer in Jesus Christ, I have given thousands to the Lord as seed offerings. I also have given away beautiful household items just because I love Jesus so much. It is my way of expressing my gratitude to Him for all the good things He has done for me.

Soon after my salvation, I went job hunting so I could provide for my growing family and the Lord gave me a good job at the light company. However, I did not like that job simply because I wanted to work at the newly opened alcohol rehab center so I applied for the job and got it. I enjoyed giving back to the Lord by ministering to the rehab clients who suffered from alcoholism.

At the end of my one-year sobriety, all the rehab clients and staff gave me a surprise party and a beautiful gift of gold earrings with a design of an animal. It was not only beautiful but also expensive. I think it was 18k gold. One Sunday afternoon, standing in the foyer of our church chatting with my friends, I suddenly felt my ear lobes as if they were on fire. I cuffed my ears with my hands and yelled out. Then I heard the Holy Spirit say to me in a commanding voice, "Take those earnings off!" I immediately did what He said and put them in my pocket. When I went home, I never asked the Lord why He said that to me. I simply forgot about the incident.

Wind That Fans The Flame

CHAPTER 6

MY BATTLE WITH THE FORCES OF WITCHCRAFT

The Dead Mouse

Mike was scrubbing the front entryway of our home with a strong detergent to remove a horrible odor but after the porch dried, the putrid odor lingered. After all that scrubbing how could that nauseating smell still be there? Where was it coming from? We looked in all the corners and under the porch and still we could not find its source. Mike gave up and came indoors to help me with the housework and prepare dinner. I was still weak from surgery and weighed just over 100 pounds but I pushed myself to do my share of the work of taking care of our four daughters.

Lately, I felt overwhelmed trying to juggle working full time at the Capitol Building and being a good mother and wife. Because of the mounting problems we were having with all of our daughters, I started to miss a Sunday service here and Wednesday night services and soon none of us were going to church anymore. Had I known how to conduct spiritual warfare against the demons assigned to destroy our family, we would not have gone through most of the trials we encountered. Neither Mike nor I knew how to fight the unseen forces arrayed against us.

One day I stopped at the music store and bought cassettes of tribal music. I love music and I thought the songs would console me but the more I listened to that type of music the more despondent I became. I do not know why I bought that style of music. When I was a new believer, I threw away about 100 records that represented the dark world of rock and roll and now I am listening to tribal music?

Lured into deception, I went to a doctor to get some medication to "calm my nerves" instead of going to the Lord for help. However, the meds did nothing except mask some of the pain I felt over my daughters' rebellion. Day after day, there was a new problem, a new crisis facing us. I felt like I was sinking deeper and deeper into despair. I could not overcome this horrible oppression in my mind, so one day ... I simply gave up. I walked into the bathroom, opened the cabinet and took the entire bottle of pills. I looked at myself in the mirror and I saw a sad face full of remorse, but I just did not care anymore. I turned and went to bed.

I had been in my bedroom for a couple of hours

when one of my daughters sensed something was wrong, so she called my friend, Kathy, who is a nurse. She quickly drove to the house and called an ambulance and Mike. Kathy rode in the ambulance with me and Mike took his own vehicle. On the way to the hospital, I stopped breathing. Kathy did mouth-to-mouth resuscitation, got me to take a deep breath, and then continued the resuscitation. All the while, she was trying to save my life, I was screaming in my mind, but I could not speak so she did not hear my scream. Once in the hospital, the doctor inserted a tube and I was on a respirator in Intensive Care, not concerned whether I lived or died.

The next morning my pastor came to see me and all he could say was, "Flo, why?" I felt so empty and void of emotion, I could not respond to him. After a couple days, I woke up to the sound of the respirator and the machine infuriated me so, I reached up and ripped the tube out of my throat. The nurse tried to stop me, but it was too late. Amazingly, I could now breathe on my own, so the medical staff moved me out of Intensive Care to a private room. I did not want any visitors, so the nurse removed my name from the outside door. One of the nurses was a Christian and she came into my room, spoke kindly with me, and left a piece of paper to read. After she left, I read it and it was a "Letter from Jesus" telling me how much He loved me. The dam of pent up emotions cracked and I wept before the Lord. I asked Him why He allowed me to live and He answered me with a Scripture:

> *Do you not know that your body is the temple of the Holy Spirit who is in you, whom you have from God, and you are not your own? For you were bought at a price; therefore glorify God in your body and in your spirit, which are God's.* (1 Corinthians 6:19-20)

After the doctor discharged me, I got my heart right with the Lord and went back to church. One day I was standing in front of our kitchen and looking at the beautiful snow-capped mountains with the snow blowing at the top and these thoughts came to me that my life is just like the turmoil at the top of that mountain so I quickly grabbed a pen and began to write.

MY LIFE
The snow-capped mountain standing alone
Without life, lonely, cold, rigid
Unmoving except for the storm that rages on
   the crest
The season passes, the sun bursts forth

> *The passivity of the snow and ice change as*
>   *streaks of rippling streams flow down*
>   *her face,*
>   *cleansing, purifying*
> *Carrying away with it the garbage of*
>   *accumulated filth of past season*
> *As the pleasant turmoil of change is over*
>   *another begins—heaving, pushing,*
>   *lifting the burden*
> *In thunderous travail, a blade penetrates*
> *Then liberty*
> *Bending, bowing in submission*
> *The winds carry past my nostrils*
> *The beauty of the flower—it touches me—*
> *I gaze at the wonder of this transformation*
>   *of new life—and stand in awe of the*
>   *Creator!*

I continued to work at our capitol, but I became increasingly dissatisfied and began to talk to the Lord about my employment. I told Him I gave the best hours of my day to my employer, but I wanted to serve Him with my whole being, with all the hours of each day. While I was in this time of reflection, Mike came home one day from work and announced we had to move to another community that had more longshoremen's work.

I was more than ready to move from the place that had so many painful memories for all of us.

We put our humble home up for sale, despite the fact our community was in a slump and homes in our area were just not selling. I made it a matter of prayer and the Lord told me it would sell within three months and we would be able to move to Ketchikan and have a new beginning. When we signed the sales contract on our home, it was 89 days after we put it on the market that it sold! It was one day short of three months.

We have moved so many times we had become expert movers, so Mike brought the boxes home and with joy we started packing. Everything was going smoothly until we moved our queen size bed and lifted the mattress. Right in the middle of the floor was the skeleton of a mouse ... and its skin and fur lay a few inches away from the skeleton! First, it is impossible for the fur to separate from the animal like that. While we were staring at it in unbelief, the Holy Spirit reminded us of the putrid odor on the porch. That was when we started having all our family problems. Finally, we knew what we had been dealing with. A demon sent to kill me and destroy our family failed in its assignment. How good is our God! I rejoiced at the grace of the Lord in saving us from the witchcraft curse of death.

You might ask how that could happen to a Christian, but the Word tells us of the warnings that we need to be aware of in 1 Peter 5:8-9:

Be sober, be vigilant; because your adversary the devil walks about like a roaring lion, seeking whom he may devour. Resist him, steadfast in the faith, knowing that the same sufferings are experienced by your brotherhood in the world.

Some Christians claim the power of the Blood of Jesus as their protection, but Jesus tells us we are protected when we obey Him. Jesus asked this question: *"Why do you call Me 'Lord, Lord,' and do not do the things which I say?"* (Luke 6:46)

I was calling Jesus my "Lord" without obeying Him, so I was a hypocrite, therefore, I could not claim the protecting power of the Blood. I did not meet His conditions, but thank God for His amazing grace. Peter, the apostle, tells us in 1 Peter 1:2, *"the elect according to the foreknowledge of God the Father, in sanctification of the Spirit, for **obedience** and sprinkling of the blood of Jesus Christ."* I knew the Holy Spirit did not approve of the tribal music but I disobeyed His still, small voice in my spirit. Because of my rebellion and disobedience, I not only suffered, but I brought misery upon my family for which I have now repented.

The Holy Spirit will dwell in a vessel that is

not totally clean, but only if you have given Him your heart. Remember when David sinned when he had an adulterous affair with Bathsheba and subsequently had her husband killed? In 2 Samuel 11, you can read the story in its entirety. Nathan the prophet confronted David with his sins, and David repented and cried out to the Lord not to take His Presence from him. His prayer is recorded in Psalm 51:11-12:

> *Do not cast me away from Your presence, and do not take Your Holy Spirit from me. Restore to me the joy of Your salvation, and uphold me by Your generous Spirit.*

David asked God not to take the Holy Spirit from him. David lost the joy of salvation and he prayed for it to be restored, but he had never lost the presence of the Holy Spirit because he could still hear the voice of Holy Spirit convicting him.

The Holy Spirit calls us to a life of separation and holiness. In 2 Corinthians 6: 17-18:

> *I will dwell in them and walk among them. I will be their God, and they shall be My people. Therefore, come out from among them and be separate, says the Lord. Do not touch what is unclean, and I will receive you. I will be a Father to you, and you shall be My sons and daughters, says the Lord Almighty.*

Then in the next verse which is 2 Corinthians 7:1 it says,

Therefore, having these promises beloved, let us cleanse ourselves from all filthiness of the flesh and spirit, perfecting holiness in the fear of God.

"Let us cleanse ourselves ... " We have to do it for ourselves. We have to repent, and then meet God's requirement for forgiveness and cleansing. The reason the Holy Spirit continued to dwell in the Apostle Paul and the Christians he was writing to, was their heart of love for the Lord Jesus Christ. We have to join in with Paul and declare, *"Not that I have already attained, or am already perfected, but I press on ... "* (Philippians 3:12-15)

I like the old saying, "The Holy Spirit does not come to indwell us because we are already perfect. He comes to help us so that we may become perfect." Amen!

Wind That Fans The Flame

CHAPTER 7

MY CALL INTO FULL TIME MINISTRY

Women's Aglow

Mike helped tie up the tour ship and the tourists flocked to downtown Ketchikan to shop and sightsee all the beauty surrounding the "Gateway City" of Alaska, which is known as the Salmon Capital of the World. Everyone seemed happy because the sun was shining. Ketchikan has almost 13 feet of rain yearly so when the sun breaks through, everyone goes out to "catch a few rays."

We finally settled into our newly purchased home in Bear Valley and found a friendly church to attend. I made friends quickly and invited them to my home for prayer, fellowship and coffee. I shared with the women how the Lord used me to help organize Women's Aglow in Juneau and we prayerfully decided to form a chapter in Ketchikan.

We made plans for the leader of the Alaskan Aglow organization to meet the potential leaders and help us organize. Once the officers were selected, and a date set for our first public meeting, we brought out the food and coffee to celebrate the new chapter. The conversation was light and the laughter loud.

When the meeting was winding down, the newly elected president made a casual comment about the totem poles in Saxman. She said when she moved to the city, she took her daughter to see the totems and the daughter said, "Oooo Mommy, there is evil in them!" When she made that comment, my smile dropped, and I was instantly enraged. I yelled at her, "What is it with you white people that you always call our totems evil, when you know nothing about our culture!" (Those were not my exact words but the content is correct.) The rest of the women looked at me in stark disbelief and the party was over. They quietly gathered their coats and said a weak goodbye and left. I was mortified at my outburst! I had no idea I felt so strongly about my culture.

For days, I was in a melancholy mood and not even Mike could console me. The joy of the Lord left me and I was under the Hand of the Lord for correction and discipline. I remained pensive for a week and finally revelation of what happened that day began to dawn on me as I sought the Lord with my whole heart. He spoke to me from John 15:1-2, 5:

"I am the true vine, and My Father is the

> *vinedresser. Every branch in Me that does not bear fruit He takes away, and every branch that bears fruit He prunes, that it may bear more fruit."*
>
> *(Verse 5) "I am the vine, you are the branches. He who abides in Me, and I in him, bears much fruit; for without Me you can do nothing."*

The Word began to wash the filth hidden deep inside of me. The Holy Spirit told me my anger towards my friend, Lynda, was unfounded. He said she was not the one trying to change me but it was *the Father ... who is the vinedresser*. He further explained when you prune a branch you cut just behind the part that is dead and useless, into the part that has the beginning of life in it. That part is not pleasant indeed, and if you resist the pruning, it will be more painful for you.

I had a stronghold in my mind that was affecting my walk with the Lord. According to Webster's New Dictionary, the word "stronghold" is a place having strong defenses, a fortress. The Lord Himself dislodged that fortress in me that was heavily guarded, that I defended with that outburst of anger. The Holy Spirit began to show me some items I had in my home that I must get rid of. I will not tell you what I got rid of because it is intensely personal. I believe every culture in the world has *stuff* and some of it beautiful and expensive, but when the God of heaven tells you to get rid of them, you should obey if you call Him Lord.

> *You shall burn the carved images of their gods with fire; you shall not covet the silver or gold that is on them, nor take it for yourselves, lest you be snared by it; for it is an abomination to the Lord your God. Nor shall you bring an abomination into your house, lest you be doomed to destruction like it. You shall utterly abhor it, for it is an accursed thing.* (Deuteronomy 7:25-26)

I went from room to room gathering objects the Holy Spirit put His finger on and He would say, "Burn this but you can keep that." I took the objects outside and burned some items and the rest I took to our garage. I grabbed Mike's sledgehammer and broke the remaining objects into many pieces. When I was finished I slumped onto the floor and cried out, "Now, Lord, I am a woman without a people; now, Lord I am a woman without a country; now Lord, I am nothing!"

Just as soon as I said that, the garage door opened and Mike did a quick look around at the broken items and exclaimed, "What the … " and he stopped and added, "Flo, don't let these women do this to you."

I said through hot tears flowing down my cheeks, "No Mike, the women did not do this to me, the Lord did."

The next day I put on a tape of worship and began to adore Him and slowly my joy and peace returned. I remained in an attitude of worship for about six months and one day while standing near the living room window, the Lord spoke ever so clearly to me and called me into full time ministry. My mind went back to the first calling when Bro. Sears spoke prophetically to me and the second time was during a Bible school class. The teacher began to quote from the call of Paul into the ministry in Acts 26:15-18: *"I am Jesus whom you are persecuting. But rise and stand on your feet; for I have appeared to you for this purpose, to make you a minister ... to open their eyes, in order to turn them from darkness to light, and from the power of Satan to God that they may receive forgiveness of sins and an inheritance among those who are sanctified by faith in Me."* Those were my words too.

I called my friends and told them I had something to share with them and when I arrived at their home, I blurted out the call of God on my life and they looked at me as if to say, "Now Flo, you are joking, right?" Nevertheless, I was undaunted and began to prepare for full time ministry. That was 31 years ago when I "put my hands to the plow," and I have never looked back.

CHAPTER 8

THE LAST DAYS CHURCH

A New Day is Dawning!

The name "Enoch" means "dedicated." It says in Genesis 5:24, *"Enoch walked with God."* Moreover, in Genesis 6:9 it says, *"Noah walked with God."* While reading that portion of Scripture, the Lord spoke to me and asked, "Did you notice *they* walked with Me?

Then I heard Amos 3:3 *"Can two walk together, unless they are agreed?"* Before I answered, He whispered to me, "I am not going to come into agreement with your thoughts, Flo, nor your ways, and the way *you* think things should be done. No, you must come into agreement with Me, *then* we can walk together."

When my journey began with the Lord Jesus Christ He showed me His endearing love, His bountiful prosperity and His gentle guidance. However, the longer I know the Lord the more He disciplines me. I have one abiding impression from my last season and it is this: Do not trifle with God!

The Word declares our *"God is a consuming*

fire." (Hebrews 12:29) He is not *like a consuming fire* ... *"No! He is a consuming fire."*

Holiness is not optional, and sanctification is not a dirty word. No believer will be a part of the bride of Christ in a manifest way unless you are clean. The purpose of sanctification is not to make you "holier than thou" but to reveal Jesus as the One who sanctifies. The Word says we are a "holy nation"—that is our distinguishing mark as a Christian—holiness—in other words, like Christ, in all our conduct.

> *But as He who called you is holy, you also be holy in all your conduct ...* (1 Peter 1:15)

The floods of adversity come to every generation but if we build our house on the rock—The Rock, Christ Jesus—our house will stand when others fall. The latter rain also comes to this generation but our walls are built with *"untempered mortar"* (Ezekiel 22:28) which will not stand the test of time; it will break and crumble when the floods of adversity come. In the Book of Revelation, it tells us the New Jerusalem's wall will be of polished jasper and these walls will be for eternity. They will not crumble, they will not crack, for the wall is made up of believers who have not compromised and have endured to the end.

> *By faith he [Moses] forsook Egypt [the world] not fearing the wrath ... for he endured ... [How?] By seeing Him who is invisible.* (Hebrews 11:27)

Hebrews 10:14 tells us sanctification is not quick and easy but a continual process, *"For by one offering He has perfected forever those who are being sanctified."*

Jesus sanctifies us ... *"with His own blood"* ... (Hebrews 13:12)

In addition, He sanctifies us by His Word, *"I do not pray that You should take them out of the world, but that You should keep them from the evil one. They are not of the world, just as I am not of the world. Sanctify them by Your truth. Your word is truth."* (John 17:15-17)

We are coming to the end of this age and the bride has made herself ready.

> *But the path of the just is like the shining sun that shines ever brighter unto the perfect day.* (Proverbs 4:18)

A wonderful teacher said "God works in you; then, you have to work it out. If you don't work out what God works in, then God will not go on working in you."

When the Word convicts us and we comply with the Holy Spirit's promptings, we will grow quickly. In Philippians 2:12-13, *"Therefore, my beloved, as you have always obeyed, not as in my presence only, but now much more in my absence, work out your own salvation with fear and trembling, for it is God who works in you both to will and to do for His good pleasure."*

If we do not work out what God has worked in, He will be grieved and not work in you until you are willing to cooperate with Him. The Lord is waiting on us to walk with Him so He can pour out His last day's "harvester's anointing" to bring in the lost and dying.

> *The last day's church will emerge " ... out of the womb of the morning ... in the beauty of holiness ... you* [will] *have the dew* [the anointing] *of your youth."* (Psalms 110:3)

A few years ago, I had a vision about the last days church. The vision takes place in the early morning just before the sun rose on the horizon. I felt warm bodies all around me and then I felt us bouncing and realized we were in the back of a flatbed truck. I kept blinking my eyes for they felt strange, small, like I was squinting. As the sun rose, I could faintly make out whom the others were and then I saw them clearly—they were sheared lambs that had given their wool for the good of another. Then I looked down at myself and I too was one of those sheared lambs. No wonder my eyes felt squinty … they were lambs' eyes. The truck was exactly the kind that takes migrant workers out into the fields to begin their long day of harvesting. I turned and saw the man sitting behind the wheel … and it was The Holy Spirit! He turned and said to me, "Flo, did you notice you are not in the driver's seat?" Smiling I said, "Yes, Lord." "Moreover, I am taking you to the field of My choice to work in the hot sun … for a new day is dawning and the harvest is ripe."

> *And this gospel of the kingdom will be preached in all the world as a witness to all the nations, and then the end will come.* (Matthew 24:14)

Wind That Fans The Flame

UPCOMING SEQUEL!

Several years ago I went to Israel and stood on the bedrock on the Temple Mount in Jerusalem. This bedrock is the only area that has never been covered with a foundation. It is the place where Abraham sacrificed his son Isaac. It is a small area that Christians from all over the world stand upon to pray for their nation. It was my turn and I had no 'prepared' prayer but the moment my feet touched the rock, I started weeping and interceding for my Native American people.

When I finished, an unknown prophet (unknown to me) came and stood directly in my face and with fire in his eyes he said to me with a rebuke, "When are you and your people going to take your place in destiny and help bring revival to America?"

CHIEF WALKIN' TALL, the sequel to *WIND THAT FANS THE FLAME*, will be released in the near future. It will be the continuing saga of a forgotten people as they take their place in destiny to help bring revival to America.

Contact Information:

DR. FLO ELLERS
PO Box 8061
Lacey, WA 98509-8061

Email:
floellers153@gmail.com